Smishing Minefield

Defusing Text Message Threats

Brett Mitchell

Copyright © 2024 Brett Mitchell

All rights reserved

The characters and events portrayed in this book are fictitious. Any similarity to real persons, living or dead, is coincidental and not intended by the author.

No part of this book may be reproduced, stored in a retrieval system, or transmitted in any form or by any means, electronic, mechanical, photocopying, recording, or otherwise, without the express written permission of the publisher.

Printed in the United States

Smishing Minefield: Defusing Text Message Threats

Table of Contents

Introduction 4
   What is Smishing? 5
Understanding Smishing Techniques 8
   Spoofing and Impersonation 11
   URL Manipulation 11
   Social Engineering Tactics 12
Recognizing Smishing Attacks 14
   Common Signs of a Smishing Message 15
   Red Flags to Watch For 16
Protecting Yourself from Smishing 18
   Keeping Phone Software Updated 19
   Verifying URLs before clicking 19
Responding to Smishing Attempts 21
Conclusion 23

Brett Mitchell

Introduction

Smishing, a portmanteau of "SMS" and "phishing", is an expanding serious threat that is making waves. A phishing attack that's carried out through SMS also known as text message, the unassuming nature of a simple text belies the disastrous potential of such attacks. Often carrying a malicious URL or phone number, the intention is to dupe the receiver into clicking on the URL or calling the number, where they will then be prompted to input sensitive information such as passwords, ID numbers, and credit card details.

Alternatively, the URL may download a type of malware onto the phone. Although such attacks have been in existence since the early 2000s, the last five years have seen smishing attacks gain increasing prevalence and success. This can be attributed to the popularity of mobile phones and the trust we place in them. In general, people are more cautious about clicking on links when using computers than on their phones, and mobile phones are more likely to be on and within easy reach at any given time.

Moreover, URL shortening services used by the likes of Twitter make it easier for a malicious URL in a text message to hide its true destination–after all, a link character count does not betray its destination. Smishing attacks frequently succeed by exploiting our inherent trust in daily communications. However, the lack of widespread awareness, due in part to insufficient action from authorities and mobile network providers, keeps smishing as a relatively obscure method of attack. The reputation and phone number of a legitimate business can be seriously and lastingly damaged if it is used in such an attack; therefore, it is important for said entities to be aware of the threat. As such, the necessity of this guide is clear–not only are individuals increasingly likely to become victims of such attacks, but also workers and leadership teams may not understand the actual risks of a successful smishing attempt. By delving into what smishing is and the differing forms it can take, the anonymity that such attacks seek to exploit can be eroded, and the general know-how to identify and respond to potential threats can be raised.

The prevention of smishing attacks lies not only in the technical protection of users, such as secure operating systems and installing antivirus software on phones, but also, crucially, in the education of vigilance and caution. However, if you use the internet with a combination of secure data, software, and good practice, your life online will be a great deal safer from the most common cybersecurity threats.

What is Smishing?

Smishing is a type of cyber attack that is carried out through SMS or text messages. As with phishing, which uses emails to lure victims into providing confidential information, smishing uses the same approach, but is dependent on the text message function that is available on most people's mobile phones. Most users trust their mobile phones, and usually, the instructions in the text message demand immediate attention. It is unusual for an average person to become suspicious.

Smishing has become more of a concern for the population today, as the shift from desktops and landline telephones to smartphones continues. This type of attack has proven to be very profitable for criminals and, as a result, has been growing significantly over the past few years. Cyber criminals who use smishing attack techniques do so for financial gain. Whether to obtain confidential information to steal the victim's identity or to access the bank and credit card accounts directly, the impact on individuals can be significant and widespread. Attacks can come in many guises, such as text messages about prize wins, requests to urgently update apparently outdated software, or confirmation of a payment to a retailer. It is often very difficult for people to spot a smishing attack, especially as attackers can deceptively change the sender/caller ID to appear as if it originated from a recipient may trust. This means that the recipient may be more likely to believe the attacker and communicate and act upon the instructions received in the smishing message. To further confuse and deceive the recipient, the message will typically give them a very limited amount of time to act and respond. This sense of urgency is a typical trait of many smishing attacks. This urgent action that the message requires is designed to try to stop the recipient from taking the time to stop and think about what is being asked of them and so not realize that the message might not be all that it seems.

An average of approximately 456 billion text messages are sent and received in the US each day. This contrasts with only 16.7 million people in the US who fall victim to smishing attacks per year, suggesting that smishing is not currently as widespread or as successful as other attack vectors. However, as more and more people become aware of phishing and the threats it presents, attackers are increasingly turning to other, less well-known methods.

The National Institute of Standards and Technology, a cybersecurity think tank and federal agency, supports this. It commented in 2018 that "SMS should not be used as a two-factor authentication method" as it was proven to be ineffective in preventing unauthorized account access. Wi-Fi Region, an online technology news platform, found that just under half of security professionals in the US had experienced a smishing attempt and that 66% of people were not even aware of what "smishing" was. This is a worryingly high figure and highlights the need for further awareness and research into SMS-focused phishing attacks. The same research also found that 57% of Americans had personally received a smishing message, which is much higher than the number of cases reported to the Federal Trade Commission in 2017. This discrepancy between the number of people who report receiving smishing messages and the number of attacks reported to law enforcement is something that is frequently seen in cybersecurity in general and is an area of great concern across all types of attacks.

The America's Health Insurance Plans and the Blue Cross Blue Shield Association have both fallen victim to and acknowledged data breaches resulting from emailing, whereas the same cannot be said for health insurance companies known to have experienced smishing attacks. This is most likely because the attackers can remain undetected and are secure in the knowledge that their attack has worked. This is even though the American Medical Informatics Association asserts that email security is one of the top five cyber priorities within clinical practice. Efforts to raise awareness of smishing are necessary, and the potential for significant damage to be done if gone undetected should encourage further research and promotion of such work in the US and across the world.

Brett Mitchell

Understanding Smishing Techniques

SMS "spoofing" and Email-to-SMS Attacks: Many SMS gateways provide the ability to modify the SMS header and provide the ability to force the sender's number to be a number (such as a short code). In addition, many gateways allow users to set the source address of an email message to an address other than their own.

These services are often marketed for commercial use to send messages using a company brand. However, if the wrong message is sent, this branding function could equally be used by an attacker who wishes to send spoofed SMS messages. This type of attack is often referred to as email -to-SMS and takes advantage of the fact that a user can send an e-mail to a mobile phone by including the mobile number within the email address, for instance, 01234456789@asnemail.com. The SMS message is transmitted to the mobile phone as if it were sent by the phone defined in the email address. Detecting SMS text messages and email to SMS spoofing is a difficult task as there is no easy method that ensures that a message is from a genuine source.

Organizations are heavily reliant on customer feedback to identify any possible problems, and it is recommended that service providers produce an abuse contact number to allow instances of suspected spoofing to be reported. Such practices can also be used to mitigate the risk of email-to-SMS spoofing attacks.

Email to SMS, sometimes known as SMS or e-mail gateway, allows users to send SMS messages to a phone using e-mail. The user can send an SMS message using an e-mail client and can include any content that e-mail supports. The messages are sent to a short code and then subsequently sent (after being translated to SMS format) to a given phone number.

SMS "spoofing" (alter the sender's information on a text message so the receiver will not know the real sender of the message) is a technology that uses the short message service (SMS), available on most mobile phones and personal digital assistants, to set who the message appears to come from by replacing the originating mobile number with alphanumeric text.

Unlike email spoofing, where a sender can enter different email addresses that have no clear ties to the recipient's address, SMS text messages can be easily spoofed (or faked) using a variety of means, and the sender's contact information can be hidden or masked. In fact, there are two possible targets of SMS text message spoofing attacks that involve sending SMS text messages to users.

In this example, a criminal is offering a fake job. There are two common motivations for this type of smishing.

Criminals are looking to obtain your personal information including bank account information.

They will mail you a check to purchase your work equipment and return a specific portion of the money back to them. Usually in the form of gift cards.

The hope is that you deposit the check and send them the remaining money before your bank notifies you the check did not clear.

Text of the message:

> Hello, we've noticed that your background and resume have been recommended by several online recruitment agencies. That's why we're offering great remote online part-time/full-time jobs to help TEMU merchants update data, increase visibility and bookings, and provide free training. Flexible part-time and full-time jobs allow you to work 60 to 90 minutes a day, 5 days a week, at flexible hours and locations (based on your own schedule), and earn $50 to $500 per day. You can earn $50 to $500 per day, with a base salary of $950 for every 4 days worked. Paid Annual Leave: In addition to maternity, paternity and other legal holidays. Regular employees are entitled to 5-15 days of paid annual leave, all paid on the same day. If you would like to participate, please contact us via WhatsApp!+14375318240

From: p1y3pjrsg5oe8b@hotmail.com

- Sender did not bother to try and obfuscate the Gmail address it came from.
- The message is generic and the sender is requesting to be contacted on the encrypted messaging application "WhatsApp".

Spoofing and Impersonation

Similar to phishing emails, smishing messages often leverage techniques such as spoofing and impersonation to manipulate users. This section details how criminals manipulate the internal and displayed properties of SMS text messages. While spoofing technically refers to the act of manipulating the header (displayed properties) of a message, most smishers also impersonate, i.e., forge the sender information. There are many ways to spoof a message. One easy way is to utilize websites that configure a message such that it uses a false "from" address. Others use a technique called "email address obfuscation". In essence, this non-standard but relatively popular technique hides the actual email addresses.

Modern smartphones tend to support multiple mobile messaging standards such as Multimedia Messaging Service or MMS. Users can send text or media on the Internet through these standards from mobile devices or personal computers using email addresses. Due to the difference in the presentation of mobile and email messages, most mobile network providers have gateway services designed to convert email messages to SMS or MMS and forward the messages to the correct mobile devices. However, this also introduces another form of spoofing under the category known as the email to SMS/MMS gateway. By configuring the "from" address field in the Internet email headers, smishers could flood many mobile devices using the weaknesses

URL Manipulation

Next, let us consider the technique known as "URL manipulation". A URL, or Uniform Resource Locator, as discussed in the previous chapter, is the address of a resource on the Internet. Most of us are familiar with the concept of a URL as we use them regularly in our web browsers. Typically, we are used to seeing URLs representing the web page that clicking on a link will take us to, and we learn to recognize the URLs that represent typical web pages, such as thepaddockparters.com are commercial sites. Those ending in ".org", such as addictionisreal.org, are not-for-profit organizations. When a victim receives a text message containing a URL, the combination of the limited amount of information that can be visible and the user's curiosity and lack of suspicion results in the victim becoming more likely to click on the link. However, in the same way that we found in Chapter 1, the sender's phone number might not always be the real sending address, so the visible text of a hyperlink will entice a click, and the actual destination might be something completely different. By creating a hyperlink (a link that the recipient of the message can click to follow), it is possible for the smisher to say anything in the hyperlink text to encourage someone to click, while still setting the link's destination to something potentially harmful. Because the linked text can say anything, and we cannot easily check on the contents of the message. In most of the commercially available operating systems for smart phones and in major PC-based web browsers, if the recipient were to hold down on the hyperlink or right-click it using a mouse and select an option to copy the link to the clipboard, then it would be possible for the recipient to inspect the true destination of the link before deciding whether to follow it. However, studies have shown that the reality is that few people actually check before clicking. Therefore, the potential for a cleverly crafted URL hyperlink to hide the true destination and present something entirely different to the victim is a very useful tool in the smisher's arsenal.

Social Engineering Tactics

Using social engineering tactics, smishers exploit human nature to manipulate and trick victims. This section explores social engineering and how it is applied in the context of smishing. Social engineering is a strategy employed by criminals to trick people into revealing confidential information. It preys on common human traits such as trust, curiosity, and the desire to help others. In the context of smishing, the goal of social engineering tactics is to deceive the recipient of a text message into taking action or providing sensitive information that could be used for malicious purposes.

Unlike the other techniques described in the previous sections, which are used to make a smishing message appear different from what it is, social engineering tactics are oriented towards getting the recipient to act in a certain way. Provoking an emotional response in the reader to cloud their judgment and convince them to do what the attacker wants. Commonly, smishers use these tactics to make the recipient feel a sense of urgency, excitement, or worry. For example, a smishing message might tell the recipient that they have won a prize and need to click on a link to claim it, generating excitement that might lead the recipient to click impulsively without thinking first. Alternatively, a message might claim that there is a problem with the recipient's bank account and that they need to click on a link immediately in order to resolve the issue, causing panic and preventing the recipient from critically analyzing the situation.

Brett Mitchell

Recognizing Smishing Attacks

Any time there is doubt regarding the legitimacy of a smashingsmishing message, you should always consult the official contact information for the organization claiming to have sent the message or call the number associated with your bank or credit card on the back of your card to reach their official customer service team. These are safe and reliable approaches to smashing detection and avoidance, as opposed to taking the bait from a suspicious message and putting your data and property at risk.

By paying attention to the characteristics of the sender and the message itself, fake messages can often be recognized. In addition, when you receive messages from unknown senders, be mindful and skeptical of the content within the message. Nowadays, almost all service providers and apps support a feature called URL preview, which shows a snapshot of the content of a link in the body of an SMS message on the phone. This can be very useful in helping you to visually identify a smishing message, as you can determine whether the link's destination is suspicious without having to physically click on the link, which might compromise your device's security. With URL preview enabled, an unknown and suspicious shortened link can usually be expanded to show the fake URL that the link actually leads to.

There is a growing trend among smashing attackers to use internet-based SMS services to send smashing messages, since it provides a way to reach large numbers of people easily and under the cover of anonymity. Such services let you send text messages to anyone from a phone number–a manipulated phone number, in the case of a smashing attacker–without making it traceable back to your identity. While such services are an important and useful part of modern internet-based communications, and they will most likely never be completely replaced by smashing-proof methods, they are currently incredibly popular among smashing attackers.

Upon receiving a smashing message, it is important to recognize that the sender is probably trying to manipulate you in some. This includes giving away sensitive information. Smishing attackers often impersonate legitimate companies or government agencies with which you are familiar , using tactics such as fear or excitement to pressure you into taking action quickly. According to the Federal Trade Commission (FTC), these attackers make the message seem urgent, hoping to trick you into making a quick response and revealing your personal information. This is why, unlike legitimate companies that really need to reach you, such as your bank or a delivery service, most of them typically do not send smashing messages. This is a major red flag and can help you identify a smashing message quite quickly.

Common Signs of a Smishing Message

A "smashing" message typically entices you to act. For example, it might say that you've won a prize, and all you need to do to claim it is reply with your name and address. Or it might say that something bad will happen unless you act immediately. For example, it might say that your bank account will be closed if you do not reply. Remember that legitimate organizations will never contact you in these ways. They will not ask you for personal information like passwords or payment details. And they certainly wouldn't threaten you. A basic sign of smashing is that the message wants you to respond by clicking on a link, calling a number, or replying with your information. Legitimate businesses will not use high-pressure tactics to obtain your personal information. Watch out for messages with a generic greeting like "dear customer". They could be smashing attempts. If a message is about your bank card or a company with which you actually have an account, the message should use your actual name. Also, look out for messages that are obviously not from the company they claim to be from. For example, if you get a message that says it's "ABC Company", really look at the message. What information are they asking for? How could a criminal use the information? If you accidentally clicked it, do not provide any information. And of course, if in doubt, contact the company, contact the company directly using the number from their website or an official bill or statement. Most companies will also provide advice about what to do if you've received a smashing message, and some will have specific phone number or email address to report it.

Red Flags to Watch For

Criminals incite a sense of insecurity in the victim in the hope that they will divulge their personal information. Hence, most of the messages of smashing will either emphasize that the victims are in peril or miss out on something significant. With the knowledge that this is a typical mind game played by the orchestrated by the criminals, victims can stay vigilant against any attempt of smashing. In addition, if there is a sense of anger in the message, this can be a red flag as well. Most of the smashing messages will attempt invoking a sense of fear, panic, or excitement. For instance, a deceptive message could falsely alert the recipient that their bank account is at risk, urging them to click a link in the message to resolve the issue promptly. Alternatively, other misleading messages may tempt the recipient with the promise of a prize or a complimentary gift, contingent upon clicking a link provided in the message. Genuine banks or service providers do not use standard network mobile numbers to send messages to their customers. When criminals use traditional numbers to send messages, it is more likely to be a smashing message, and the activity should be reported to the relevant authorities. The recipient should spend some time looking at the content of the message, inspection the URL in the message, and looking for similar messages they may have received. If something is out of place or the message is out of character, it is probably a scam. The next red flag to watch for is the economic aspect of the message. Nearly every smashing message includes a command paired with a sense of immediate urgency. For instance, it might suggest that clicking on a provided link will prevent financial losses, avoid fines, or even avert legal consequences such as jail time. Knowing these tactics are commonly employed by criminals who exploit individuals' fears, the recipients is in a much better position to defend themselves.

Brett Mitchell

Protecting Yourself from Smishing

regarding protecting yourself from smashing, one of the most straightforward yet vital steps you can take is to keep your phone software up to date. Developers release updates to fix vulnerabilities attackers exploit; therefore, failing to update your device can leave you at unnecessary risk. Both Apple and Android have frequent software updates, and in most cases, you can choose to install these as soon as they become available. However, if you are the sort of person who tends to dismiss or ignore reminders, you might want to enable automatic updates instead. In this way, you can relax knowing that your phone will always be equipped with the latest security protections. A key tip is to be wary of messages from people you don't know. We often get texts like ads, surveys, or other things from strangers. It's easy to ignore who sends these, but it's important to always be cautious of unknown senders. Vigilance is particularly important if the message asks you to disclose personal, or financial information. or if it tries to persuade you to click on an unsolicited link. However, even if neither of these tactics are present in the message, it still might be smishing. The motive for the message might not always be clear initially. In addition to these steps, it is also a good idea to verify URLs before clicking on them. In general, it is safer to avoid clicking on links in text messages unless you can be absolutely certain it is from a trusted source, even if you know the sender. Instead, enter the habit of checking websites via a search engine, or even typing the URL directly into your browser. At the very least, you should hover over the link to preview the web address and ensure that it appears legitimate. By staying cautious and making the effort to manually verify URLs, you can add an extra layer of protection against smashing attacks.

Keeping Phone Software Updated

Since older software on your phone is more likely to have a security vulnerability that attackers can exploit to access your data. So, the importance of keeping all software up to date, not just the operating system. You can usually do this through your phone settings, although it depends on the type of phone you have. Always try to ensure that you have the latest version of your phone's software, and if you no longer receive updates for your current phone, it might be time to think about getting a new one. However, itis important that you do not fall for the temptation to download updates from unofficial sources; you should only download updates from the phone manufacturer.

Verifying URLs before clicking

As mentioned in previous chapters. When you receive a text message containing a URL, whether it directs you to your bank's website for a special offer or to a local news site, it is essential that you do not click the link until you have verified it. The verification process can be quite straightforward. If the message's main body does not make sense or is written in such a way as to prompt an immediate response (such as telling you that your account is in danger of being deactivated), this should increase your suspicion and encourage you to investigate further, for example, by contacting the apparent sender directly. However, even if the message seems plausible, do not click the URL. Instead, research the true phone number and call the company to check whether they sent the message. In this way, you do not risk giving away data. You can also save the real number in your phone's contacts list under the genuine name of the company. However, companies might not always call from the same number, so that might always work. Additionally, it is not difficult for criminals to spoof caller ID. Giving the appearance of legitimacy to the recipient. For example, if you receive a call and the caller ID says it is your bank and you have your bank's number saved in your contacts. You might inadvertently believe the call is legitimate.

Responding to Smishing Attempts

As mentioned previously. If you receive a smashing message, it is important to refrain from responding or clicking on any links. Even if the message claims that your response is required to rectify an issue or to unsubscribe from further communications. Engaging in any way confirms s that your phone number is active. This may lead to increased smashing messages. Additionally, any links contained within the message should never be clicked on or followed as this can lead to your smartphone being infected with malware or the recipient being directed to a phishing website where login credentials are stolen. Instead, such messages should be promptly reported to both your mobile network provider and Federal Trade Commission (FTC). SubmissionMost providers allow smishing messages beto be sent free of charge. Here are some reporting resources.

- Copy the message and forward it to 7726 (SPAM).
    - This helps your wireless provider spot and block similar messages in the future.

- It can also be reported to the FTC at www.reportfraud.ftc.gov.
- Internet Crime Complaint Center (IC3) report smashing attempts to the IC3, which is a partnership between the Federal Bureau of Investigation (FBI) and the National White Collar Crime Centre

During the reporting process, users will be asked to provide certain details such as the time and date of the message, the phone number from which the message was sent , and the content of the message itself. It is possible to submit an anonymous report; however, the provision of detailed information is the most effective approach in assisting with the identification of the sender. By engaging with and supporting such initiatives, users play an active role in the fight against cybercrime while contributing toward a safer mobile environment for everyone.

Conclusion

As we reach the culmination of our journey through the labyrinth of SMS phishing—smishing—it's imperative to reflect on the critical insights and defensive strategies we've navigated together. This final chapter isn't merely a conclusion but a beacon for the path forward, a consolidation of our collective understanding, and a call to action in the persistent battle against smishing threats.

The essence of combating smishing lies not in the sophistication of the technology we wield but in the depth of our awareness. We've peeled back the layers of deceit employed by attackers, revealing the mechanisms of spoofing, impersonation, and URL manipulation. By recognizing these tactics, we empower ourselves to scrutinize every SMS, to question the unfamiliar, and to verify the dubious.

The narrative of smishing is one of constant evolution; as our defenses grow, so do the strategies of our adversaries. Thus, vigilance must be more than a practice—it must become a principle. The examples provided, from the benign-seeming prize notifications to the urgent financial alerts, serve as a testament to the cunning of smishers. Let these scenarios be a guide, but not a limitation, for vigilance extends beyond known patterns to the anticipation of the unforeseen.

Our defense against smishing is not solely an individual endeavor but a collective one. By educating others—friends, family, colleagues—we extend our shield, creating a network of informed users resilient to the ploys of smishers. Each conversation about smishing, each shared experience, fortifies this collective defense, making our digital ecosystem a more formidable fortress against deception.

Adopting proactive measures—keeping software updated, verifying URLs, and reporting smishing attempts—embodies the personal responsibility we hold in safeguarding our digital identity. The tools and practices outlined herein are not merely recommendations but essential components of a comprehensive defense strategy against smishing. It's through these proactive steps that we not only protect ourselves but also contribute to the broader effort of cybercrime prevention.

As we close this chapter and look to the future, let us recognize that our journey in cybersecurity vigilance is ongoing. The landscape of digital threats, smishing among them, will continue to evolve, demanding our persistent attention and adaptation. But armed with knowledge, empowered by awareness, and united in our collective defense, we stand ready to face these challenges head-on.

Let his book be a manifesto for the modern digital citizen. As we navigate the complexities of the digital age, this book serve as a compass, guiding us toward a more secure and informed digital existence. The fight against smishing is not won in a single battle but in the continual commitment to education, vigilance, and proactive defense. Together, we forge ahead, fortified in our resolve to turn the tide against smishing and secure the sanctity of our digital lives.

www.ingramcontent.com/pod-product-compliance
Lightning Source LLC
Chambersburg PA
CBHW030109230526
45471CB00003B/1331